An opinionated guide to

SECRET LONDON

written by
EMMY WATTS

Crossness Pumping Station (no.31)

INFORMATION IS DEAD. LONG LIVE OPINION.

When we conceived these guidebooks, we expected them to fail. Who needs a guidebook when everything can be Googled for free?

But then it occurred to us, that's exactly why you *do* want a guidebook. You want lively, trustworthy opinion combined with great photographs. You don't want endless information from a thousand online bots.

We think you are like us: you care about quality, you care about style, you care about provenance, but you don't have time to waste on long words like 'provenance'. You want to cut to the chase: where's good?

If you were to come and stay on our couch (it's a metaphor btw; we have a guide to hotels), these are the places we'd recommend.

Ann & Martin, co-founders
Hoxton Mini Press

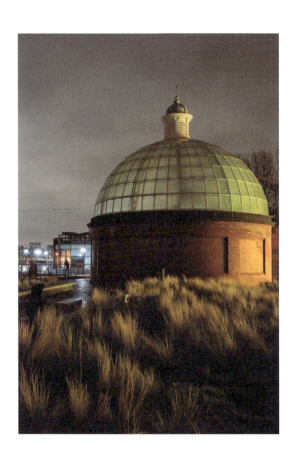

Greenwich Foot Tunnel (no.29)
Opposite: The Hill Garden and Pergola (no.55)

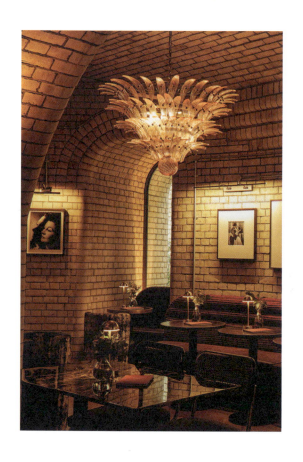

Larry's (no.3)
Opposite: Ümit & Son (no.24)

Lounge Bohemia (no.11)
Opposite: Hidden London Tours (no.1)

WANT TO KNOW A SECRET?

There's more to London than oversized Ferris wheels, misidentified clocktowers and unsmiling sentries in silly hats. Invariably overhyped and overpriced, the capital's star attractions aren't always its best bits. While most London guidebooks will blithely bundle you onto the tourist trail, this one signposts the road less trodden, shining a (surreptitious) torchlight on the city's hidden gems.

Of course, nothing is ever truly unknown in a city like London. In the age of TikTok and Instagram, a supposedly 'secret' spot pops up every week. When the hidden location of Queen's Wood's (no.57) gingerbread cottage-style cafe was revealed via a series of viral videos, staff were quickly overwhelmed. Meanwhile, word of Ümit Mesut's film club and backroom cinema (no.24) travelled from Hackney to Hollywood, allegedly piquing the interest of Quentin Tarantino and sparking talk of a documentary.

Still, many of London's superlative secrets have remained so for aeons. Did you know about the 2,000-year-old Roman amphitheatre on display in the basement of a City of London gallery (no.8)? Or that Greenwich's Old Royal Naval College is home to both the 'British Sistine Chapel' (no.30) and a fully functioning, 19th-century precursor to the modern bowling alley (no.34)? What about Great Eastern Street's longest-running secret: an underground bar conjuring molecular cocktails beneath a nondescript kebab shop since 2007 (no.11)?

Our collective craving for the covert isn't showing any sign of abating. The resurgence in Prohibition-themed speakeasies has given rise to a new wave of hidden bars that compel punters to text mysterious numbers, pass through unmarked doorways and mutter secret passwords in order to gain access.

Our fascination with the furtive comes down to our innate curiosity. Being given carte blanche to do something that feels illicit is thrilling, whether it's poking around behind normally locked doors at Open House Festival (no.7), reconnoitring once-private gardens like the secluded St John's Lodge (no.53) and crumbling Hill Garden and Pergola (no.55); or delving into the sordid history of London's enigmatic East End, courtesy of Dennis Severs' atmospheric townhouse (no.20) or a no-details-spared Jack the Ripper tour (no.18).

This is your guide to that other side of London. Your passport to rooftop gardens, underground dining rooms, secret shopping streets and many more hush-hush haunts that we might easily have kept to ourselves, but haven't – because, deep down, we know that London is a city best shared. Just keep it to yourself, okay?

Emmy Watts
London, 2025

Emmy Watts is a London-based writer and blogger. As well as writing ten other books for this series, Emmy has been divulging the capital's best-kept family-friendly secrets via her blog, bablands.com, since 2017. Despite this – and this book – she's an excellent secret-keeper.

BEST FOR...

Underground bars
Bored to tears by your go-to boozer? Shake things up with madcap mixology at Lounge Bohemia (no.11), an adventure through the bookcase at creative cocktail bar The Vault (no.38) or all-out Great Gatsby glamour at Larry's (no.3), the National Portrait Gallery's secret speakeasy.

Discreet dining
The romantic interiors of Sessions Art Club (no.12) were made for dreamy date nights. The Jackalope's (no.39) numbing noodles are as good as any you'll find in Chinatown, and the setting far more serene. Alternatively, give new meaning to the term 'blind date' at Dans le Noir (no.6).

Classified culture
The highlight of any trip to the Postal Museum, Mail Rail (no.2) offers a whistlestop tour of London's secret underground mail network. Or check out the capital's answer to the Sistine Chapel, the Old Royal Naval College's epic Painted Hall (no.30).

Secret gardens
When the urban jungle leaves you longing for an actual jungle (or at least a patch of grass and some peace), seek out Dalston Eastern Curve Garden (no.25) for its bohemian spirit or the Barbican Conservatory (no.14) for concrete and cacti.

Hush-hush history

Did you know that the Guildhall Art Gallery houses a Roman amphitheatre (no.8)? That the Hidden Underground Tour (no.1) reveals wartime Tube shelters? Or that you can engage in some light time travel by visiting Dennis Severs' House (no.20) and its two centuries of haunting secret history?

Quirky discoveries

London is chockfull of weird secrets – you just need to know where to find them. Discover a lucky-dip literary vending machine (no.44) in a Soho basement, a Victorian pet cemetery (no.47) in the corner of a Royal Park and 'Roman' mosaics (no.50) through a hidden Hackney subway.

Furtive fun

Like your entertainment with an air of mystery? How do a subterranean Skittle Alley (no.34) dating back to 1873, a 15-seat backroom cinema (no.24) operated by your own private projectionist and a secluded rooftop sauna (no.22) with panoramic views sound?

Seasonal secrets

For one weekend in June, visitors can snoop around 100+ private green spaces courtesy of London Open Gardens (no.22). In September, Open House London (no.7) flings open 800 doors to the hoi polloi. Fancy a poke around Eel Pie Island (no.15)? Look out for its Open Studios every July and December.

CENTRAL

1
HIDDEN LONDON TOURS

Illuminating underground excursions

Ghost stations and ghost stories. Bomb shelters and war bunkers. The London Underground has its fair share of secrets (it's been knocking around for 160 years, after all). Fortunately, London Transport Museum's Hidden London tours are dreadful at keeping them. So bad, in fact, that they offer not one, not two but *twelve* lively Tube tours devised expressly to reveal them. Fancy pounding the abandoned platforms at Aldwych station – shuttered 30 years ago due to scarce footfall? Or perhaps you'd prefer a poke around one of London's eight deep-level wartime shelters? Whatever your mission, expect knowledgeable guides, plenty of gossip and VIP access to restricted areas (plus 50 per cent off entry to the LTM).

Various locations
ltmuseum.co.uk/hidden-london

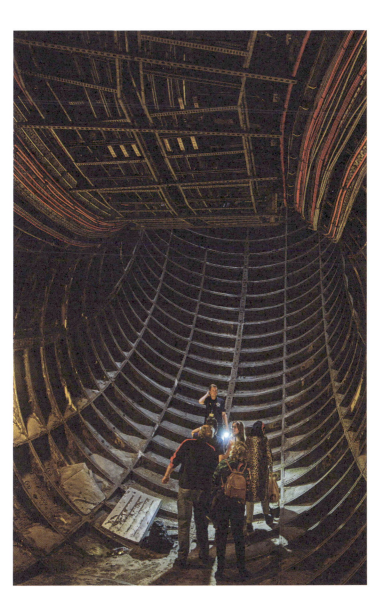

CENTRAL

2

MAIL RAIL

Subterranean miniature railway

London's Underground network might be one of the most famous on the planet, but the capital's other subterranean train service is a relative unknown – even among lifelong Londoners. Formerly the Post Office Railway, the satisfyingly renamed Mail Rail conveyed post beneath London for almost a century before rising costs and declining use stopped it in its tracks. Now part of the brilliantly interactive Postal Museum, Mail Rail has been reimagined as a charming circular train ride that runs through the tunnels under Farringdon and is accompanied by an absorbing audiovisual narrative recounting the railway's story. Its location beneath the museum's interactive children's gallery makes it especially great for families, but it's still a must for anyone with a soft spot for snail mail.

15–20 Phoenix Place, WC1X 0DA
Nearest station: Farringdon
postalmuseum.org

CENTRAL

3
LARRY'S

Swish speakeasy in gallery vault

Great Gatsby glamour abounds at Larry's, a smart but unpretentious jazz bar deep in the heart of the National Portrait Gallery. Once a run-of-the-mill cafe, and originally built as a coal store, this freshly reinvigorated space draws inspiration from the National Portrait Gallery's most celebrated sitters and photographers. Its name is an homage to actor Laurence Olivier, while the concoctions on its mouthwatering cocktail menu pay tribute to everyone from Audrey Hepburn (a delicate White Lady) to Cecil Beaton (a complex Dubonnet and gin). Theatregoers can enjoy an early evening menu pre-performance – though with its live jazz, decadent bar snacks, plush Prohibition-era decor and charismatic wait staff, this place might have all the drama you need.

National Portrait Gallery, St. Martin's Place, WC2H 0HE
Nearest station: Charing Cross
daisygreenfood.com

4
KATSUTE100

Japanese teahouse serving matcha and desserts

In a place as frenetic as Covent Garden, nothing remains secret for long. This Japanese tea shop, however, is a welcome anomaly, thanks to its covert location on the second floor of a Grade II-listed former coach house – now a massive Uniqlo. Along with full-bodied matcha and 20 soothing varieties of Japanese tea, this delightfully zen spot offers a delectable array of traditionally inspired desserts. Whether you opt for a rich and nutty black sesame souffle, creamy matcha crepe cake and a deliciously perfumed Sakura Mont Blanc tart, it's the perfect antidote to shopping in central London. And if that's still not quite hidden enough, head up on warmer days for iced matcha lattes on the restful roof terrace.

2nd Floor, Uniqlo, 19–20 Long Acre, WC2E 9LZ
Nearest station: Covent Garden
katsute100.com

CECIL COURT

Quaint cobbled street with antique bookshops

Steps from the bright lights and big screens of Leicester Square, this inconspicuous alley caters to a humbler form of entertainment. Often nicknamed Booksellers' Row owing to its throng of second-hand and antique bookstores, this quiet cut-through is a literature lover's paradise and one-stop destination for everything from the works of Lewis Carroll and signed first editions to obsolete maps and rare music manuscripts. In keeping with their merchandise, the shopfronts haven't changed in more than a century, while the shopkeepers' fastidious service only adds to the old-timey magic. Short on time? Marchpane (children's books), November Books (fashion and design) and Watkins (esoterica) are all ones to bookmark.

Cecil Court, WC2N
Nearest station: Leicester Square
cecilcourt.co.uk

CENTRAL

6
DANS LE NOIR?

Fine dining in the dark

The clue is in the name at Dans Le Noir?, an immersive dining experience where patrons devour a gourmet feast in pitch darkness. Beyond the concept, though, this place gives away tantalisingly little. Menus, like mobile phones (and lightbulbs) are forbidden in the dining room, and your meal's components are only revealed afterwards, when you are guided into the well-lit bar by your own personal member of staff. Any initial claustrophobia will dissipate with the arrival of the food – tender butternut squash gnocchi followed by meringue-crowned blackberry panna cotta, for instance – as you quickly become consumed by the need to correctly identify every morsel that touches your lips. Don't be afraid to get your hands in there – after all, no one's looking.

69–73 St John Street, EC1M 4NJ
Nearest station: Farringdon
danslenoir.com

CENTRAL

7
OPEN HOUSE

Inside London's architectural gems

Ever fancied a spin on BT Tower's revolving floor, a stroll through Trellick Tower's concrete walkways or a peek behind the scenes at Number 10? This annual architecture festival is your key to the (usually diligently guarded) doors of the capital's most enigmatic addresses. From private residences to iconic landmarks, there's something for every taste. Mad about Modernism? Tag onto a tour of Chamberlin, Powell and Bon's revered Golden Lane council housing complex, or enjoy a licit poke around Hampstead's pioneering Isokon Building – once home to famous artists, authors and spies. If you're looking for something a little more unusual, tootle down to Tooting and check out Sadiq Khan's favourite building: a bonkers bingo hall masquerading as a Russian Orthodox church.

Various locations
openhouse.org.uk

8
LONDON'S ROMAN AMPHITHEATRE

Rousing remains of a 1st-century arena

Its hoard of masterpieces, including works by Rossetti, Leighton and Constable, is reason enough to visit the Guildhall Art Gallery. Venture into its dimly lit basement, though, and you'll ponder why it's not packed with tourists – given the quiet presence of a ruined Roman amphitheatre dating to 70 CE. There's not much left of the structure beyond the ragstone walls, ancient timber drains and a small quantity of the sand that absorbed the bloodshed, but digital projections simulating the original curved seating and sparring gladiators bring it dramatically back to life. Don't miss the building's atmospheric piazza, where an arc of paving stones traces the original amphitheatre's substantial perimeter.

Guildhall Art Gallery, Guildhall Yard, EC2V 5AE
Nearest station: Bank
thecityofldn.com

9
THE POST BUILDING ROOF GARDEN

Viewing deck with spectacular vistas

You may have visited the Sky Garden, but have you experienced the giddy heights of this little-known Holborn roof terrace? Opened in 2022 following the redevelopment of the former Royal Mail sorting office, this secret spot enjoys near-panoramic views of central London that belie its petite stature – just nine stories above the ground. No pre-booking is required, but you'll need photo ID to pass through the airport-style security and ride the lift to the garden. On emerging, you'll discover a vista that stretches from the BT Tower in the northwest to the BFI in the south, with rare bird's-eye views of the British Museum's domed roof. Don't miss the spiral sorting chute in reception – a relic of the building's postie past.

29–31 New Oxford Street, WC1A 1BA
Nearest stations: Holborn, Tottenham Court Road
postbuilding.com

CENTRAL

10
THE ARTIST'S GARDEN

Tube-top terrace showcasing women artists' work

Angel station possesses the longest escalator on the network; Clapham Common and Clapham North are known for their island platforms. Temple, by contrast, boasts little to set it apart from any other Underground station – that is, until you exit left and ascend the staircase to the half-acre roof terrace dedicated to thought-provoking installations produced exclusively by women artists. Once part of London's Victorian-era engineering efforts to combat the Great Stink of 1858, the long-abandoned veranda has been revived over the past five years, hosting everything from Lakwena Maciver's rainbow-hued wonderland, to the site of a mammoth Holly Hendry pipe installation, with plenty more on the horizon. That stunning South Bank skyline is also pretty hard to beat.

Temple Station Roof Terrace, WC2R 2PH
Nearest station: Temple
thecolab.art

CENTRAL

11
LOUNGE BOHEMIA

Conceptual cocktails in a kitsch hideaway

Your average Shoreditch cocktail bar doesn't stick around for long, but then eccentric mixologist Paul Tvaroh's subterranean speakeasy is anything but average. Concealed beneath a Great Eastern Street kebab shop since 2007 (aeons, in Shoreditch years), Lounge Bohemia seems to exist in an alternate dimension – one where the decor is straight out of Communist-era Prague and the drinks are genuine magic. Whether you plump for a Prick (a madman's margarita whose flavour depends on which of the glass's custom cactus arms you drink from) or a Bearllini (an unexpectedly solid arrangement of alcoholic gummy bears), be sure to leave your suit and cynicism at the (unmarked) door. And don't even think about showing up without giving Paul a bell first.

1e Great Eastern Street, EC2A 3EJ
Nearest station: Old Street
loungebohemia.com
07720707000

CENTRAL

12
SESSIONS ARTS CLUB

Decadent dining room in old courthouse

Stepping through the unmarked door into this 300-year-old dining room feels like entering a time portal, so exquisitely preserved is what lies behind it. Ring the doorbell and climb four flights of spiral stairs before taking your seat in a lightly crumbling former judges' chambers, surrounded by peeling plasterwork, tastefully shabby armchairs and an ever-evolving gallery of contemporary art. The menu, like the art, changes with the seasons and feels just as modern: expect dishes like tantalisingly tender mussels crowned with juicy RAF tomato crowns, or perfectly poached hake cloaked in wild garlic – all washed down with a musky melon martini.

4th Floor, 24 Clerkenwell Green, EC1R 0NA
Nearest station: Farringdon
sessionsartsclub.com

CENTRAL

13
POSTMAN'S PARK

Tranquil garden honouring everyday heroes

Doubting the existence of good in this world? Set off in pursuit of this verdant walled garden, whose elusiveness belies the extraordinary acts of bravery memorialised within. Here, buried between St Paul's and the Barbican complex, lies artist George Frederic Watts' modest yet moving memorial to 62 everyday joes who surrendered their lives for others – from the nanny who perished saving her three charges from a house fire, to the ship's stewardess who gave up her lifebelt and sank with her vessel. Prettily presented on Doulton ceramic tiles, these accounts are at once heart-wrenching and heartening, making this one of the City of London's most soulful secrets.

King Edward Street, EC1A 7BT
Nearest station: St. Paul's

CENTRAL

14
BARBICAN CONSERVATORY

Brutalist bastion's indoor oasis

Social media might have betrayed the Barbican's leafy secret, but this concrete jungle remains one of the capital's most precious gems. While its sporadic opening hours haven't dimmed the conservatory's unwaning popularity with the TikTok throng, there's still endless tranquillity to be found across its intricate maze of walkways and balconies. Head here in pursuit of mammoth monsteras, colossal cacti and weeping figs so tall they require yearly pruning – and don't miss the colourful carp and terrapins who inhabit the conservatory's cold-water ponds. Book your (free) entry tickets up to a month in advance – and keep your eyes peeled for occasional afternoon teas under the glass ceiling.

Silk Street, EC2Y 8DS
Nearest station: Barbican
barbican.org.uk

CENTRAL

15

LONDON OPEN GARDENS

Unlocking the capital's private parkland

If you've always fancied a poke around one of London's residents-only garden squares – à la Hugh Grant and Julia Roberts in 1990s rom-com *Notting Hill* – consider this annual festival your free pass (minus the fence hopping). Held over a weekend in June, the open-access event sees more than 100 clandestine gardens flung open to the masses, with everything from family treasure hunts to Shakespearean shorts bringing them spectacularly to life. You won't have time to visit them all, but 25 Cannon Street's up-close views of St Paul's, the living roof garden atop Eversheds Sutherland and Rosmead Garden (the actual square used in the aforementioned the film) all make for essential viewing.

Various locations
londongardenstrust.org

EAST

16
ROCHELLE CANTEEN

Feasting in a former school bike shed

Tucked away inside a converted bike shed, within a former school, behind an unassuming gate, across a little green at the heart of the world's first social housing estate, you'll discover a restaurant you simply cannot miss. Lesser establishments would struggle in such a furtive setting, but this revered celebrity haunt is all the more treasured for its sense of seclusion, with reservations snapped up far in advance. Should you succeed in securing a table (and locating it – ring the bell for entry), order voraciously from the fun, fuss-free menu, regulars of which include seared sardines sweetened with blood orange and silky, charred aubergine enveloped in unctuous labneh. Perhaps we should have kept this one to ourselves…

16 Playground Gardens, E2 7FA
Nearest station: Shoreditch High Street
rochellecanteen.com

17
THE NATURAL PHILOSOPHER

Botanical cocktails behind a Mac repair shop

Unless you're a MacBook owner whose device is plagued by ailments, you're probably wretchedly unaware of this fun and friendly cocktail spot. Accessed via the steampunk stylings of MacSmiths repair shop and Vintage Mac museum, this is a speakeasy with a difference: a cosy slice of Victoriana where madcap concoctions are magicked up from organic liquor and locally foraged ingredients inside a sunken bar. The menu changes monthly, but the cocktails are reliably inventive: oaky apple brandy blended with aromatic gin and creamy horchata, while tangy tequila and honeyed tomato come with a sour salmonberry punch. Soak it up with a Yard Sale pizza delivered direct to your bar stool.

Inside The Macsmiths, 489 Hackney Road, E2 9ED
Nearest station: Cambridge Heath
naturalphilosopher.co.uk

18
JACK THE RIPPER TOUR

Secret history of the killer's stomping ground

Not just for the true-crime fans, these wickedly creepy walking tours will captivate anyone with a curiosity for London's secret – and frequently horrible – history. Eloquently led by genuine Jack the Ripper experts, these theatrical excursions steer guests through the atmospheric warren of narrow East End backstreets where the notorious serial killer murdered at least five female sex workers in 1888, with frequent stop-offs at the crime scenes (you'll never look at the Sunday UpMarket in the same way again) and plenty of grisly visual aids. Tours are intense and last two hours, so why not fuel up beforehand at The Ten Bells, the Spitalfields boozer allegedly frequented by victims Annie Chapman and Mary Jane Kelly.

Exit 1, Aldgate East Underground Station, Whitechapel High Street, E1 7PT
Nearest station: Aldgate East
jack-the-ripper-tour.com

19
TRINITY BUOY WHARF

Unusual cultural hub on the peninsula tip

Few pockets of London feel so surreally secluded as Trinity Buoy Wharf, a distinctive hamlet on the Leamouth Peninsula. Home to the capital's only remaining lighthouse, this curious cultural centre stands out in more ways than one, despite being far less identifiable than its neighbour, the eminent O2. Arrive via East India Quay's waterfront park for a taste of rural charm, or snake past London City Island's colourful skyscrapers, pausing to inspect the old ironworks' ghost signs. Stop for coffee (and a selfie) at the black-cab-topped Orchard Cafe before exploring the numerous offbeat attractions, from an immersive recreation of scientist Michael Faraday's study, to a 16-screen cinematic retelling of the area's history – and even a continuous musical installation beneath the lighthouse eaves that could run for the next 1,000 years.

64 Orchard Place, E14 0JW
Nearest stations: East India, Canning Town
trinitybuoywharf.com

20
DENNIS SEVERS' HOUSE

Candlelit 'time machine' in a Georgian townhouse

The secret lives of several generations of the same (fictional) family are laid bare at this spellbinding museum – a convincingly constructed 'still-life drama' that transports visitors on a hyper-sensorial journey inside an 18th-century house. The life's work of eccentric former owner and namesake Dennis Severs, who passed away in 1999, this dreamlike installation has been assembled as though it is still lived in, with everything from half-eaten plates of remarkably realistic food (complete with bite marks) to unmade beds and still-crackling fires, at times making for an uneasy encounter. Whether you opt for the revealing guided or atmospheric silent tour, few museum experiences are as captivating (or smelly).

18 Folgate Street, E1 6BX
Nearest station: Shoreditch High Street
dennissevershouse.co.uk

21
THE VIKTOR WYND MUSEUM OF CURIOSITIES

Perverse paraphernalia in bar basement

There's good reason this compendium of 'curiosities' is buried beneath a kooky-looking absinthe bar. Comprising, among other horrors, a syphilitic wax penis, a stool sample purportedly collected from Kylie Minogue and used condoms allegedly pilfered from the Rolling Stones' hotel room, the artist's ghoulish hoard isn't one you'd care to stumble upon accidentally – and a pre-visit tipple probably wouldn't go amiss. The authenticity of some exhibits is debatable (ever encountered a fully articulated mermaid skeleton?) but that's all part of Viktor Wynd's particular brand of fun. Speaking of which, the museum's Witchy Wednesdays workshops are unnervingly excellent.

11 Mare Street, E8 4RP
Nearest station: Cambridge Heath
thelasttuesdaysociety.org

EAST

22
ROOFTOP SAUNAS

Scenic sweating

There's only one thing better than your own private sauna – and that's your own private sauna with knockout views of the London skyline. Iconic rooftop bar Netil360 might be far from mysterious after popping up above the chimneys of London Fields more than ten years ago, but its founders' latest venture on the adjacent roof feels infinitely more covert. A backstreet entrance, intercom access and minimalist signposting all add to the vibe – not to mention its cosy private cabins, which can accommodate four friends for up to 90 blissful minutes. Once you're all sweated and cold-plunged out, simply hop through the gate for drinks, pizza, DJs and plenty more of those jaw-dropping views.

Netil Corner, 2 Bocking Street, E8 4RU
Nearest station: London Fields
rooftopsaunas.com

23
THE APPROACH GALLERY

Pint-sized gallery above a welcoming pub

Commercial galleries are notorious for their subtle signposting, but this inspiring Bethnal Green gem is particularly tricky to find – accessed only by means of a 'secret' staircase inside a Victorian boozer of the same name. Thankfully for founder Jake Miller, that doesn't seem to have done The Approach any harm. If anything, its location is one of the gallery's main allures, with art lovers flocking here in pursuit of both a pint and The Next Big Thing. A formidable force in launching the careers of fledgling artists (Sara Cwynar and Sandra Mujinga are both recent alumnae), this tiny two-room gallery is just as renowned for its intergenerational group shows, often guest-curated by legends of the art world. Approach *without* caution.

1st Floor, 47 Approach Road, E2 9LY
Nearest station: Bethnal Green
theapproach.co.uk

24
ÜMIT & SON

Celluloid film shop with a private screening room

Ümit Mesut Hassan is fanatical about film – a fact advertised by his Hackney movie store's memorabilia-stuffed windows. 'Digital is getting better, but it's still shit compared with film,' proclaims Mesut, who's presided over this cave of cinematic wonders for more than 35 years. While the shop itself is easily missed thanks to its faded frontage, it's Mesut's 15-seat backroom cinema that's the real hidden gem. The exclusively private screenings include full access to his encyclopaedic 16mm film library – as well as access to Mesut himself for all your projection needs. Just BYOB and he'll provide the popcorn (and the movie magic).

35 Lower Clapton Road, E5 0NS
Nearest station: Hackney Central
cine-real.com

25
DALSTON EASTERN CURVE GARDEN

Urban oasis with a cafe and events

When the cacophony of Kingsland Road leaves you craving calm, swerve into the Curve. Cultivated on what was once the Eastern Curve Railway line that connected Camden to Poplar, this fairy-tale Dalston oasis has flourished into the very definition of a community garden. Over 15 years, it's hosted everything from lively social clubs for older people, to interactive music classes for toddlers, not to mention an on-site cafe serving some seriously addictive cake. Easy to miss amid the hubbub of Dalston, the Curve is filled with twinkling fairy lights and mulled wine-sipping revellers in winter, and the bolstering hum of live music and frolicking families from spring onwards, when the motley assortment of ride-ons brings all the kids to the yard.

13 Dalston Lane, E8 3DF
Nearest station: Dalston Junction
dalstongarden.org

SOUTH

26
EEL PIE ISLAND

Private artist community with rock 'n' roll past

You'll struggle to find pie on this enigmatic island, but if you're in the market for an intoxicating dose of rock 'n' roll history and more original art than you can shake a bag of eels at, it might be time you paid a visit (though that's easier said than done). Once home to the UK's largest hippie commune, this magical mudflat retains much of its bohemian charm thanks to its vibrant artist community who, for two weekends a year, welcome the masses as part of Artists Open Studios. While the commune (and Pink Floyd) is long gone, there's still lots to see – keep an eye on their Instagram account for information on open-days and visit the (mainland) museum in the meantime.

TW1 3DY
Nearest station: Twickenham
eelpieislandartists.co.uk

SOUTH

27

WC WINE & CHARCUTERIE

Intimate bar in a Victorian toilet

Seeking a drinking den with a difference? Look no further than this former gents' toilet – which is thankfully no longer in the business of letting men... do their business. But despite serving fine wine, classic cocktails and meaty morsels beneath Clapham Common tube station for more than a decade, this low-lit bar still upholds the spirit (though thankfully not the smell) of the old Victorian restroom. Everything from the ceramic tiles to the wooden toilet stalls surrounding the booths is a painstakingly restored original. Order a peachy pinot grigio or a velvety Negroamaro, then soak it all up with a princely pile of expertly sourced charcuterie and a gooey wheel of camembert.

Clapham Common South Side, SW4 7AA
Nearest station: Clapham Common
Other locations: Bloomsbury
wcbars.co.uk

28
BONNINGTON SQUARE

Vauxhall 'village' with notable history

Desperately seeking an antidote to the horrors of the Vauxhall gyratory? Find it in this serene Victorian square, whose village vibes and dense foliage defy its inner-city setting. On the brink of demolition in the 1980s, the square was subsequently inhabited by an ambitious community of squatters, who established the verdant 'pleasure' garden and vegetarian cafe that endure today. Now well established, the garden is all exotic rambling plants and noise-blocking trees, while an ever-changing roster of inspirational chefs flows through the cafe's kitchen, dishing up delectable fare from every corner of the Earth. Text ahead to guarantee a table, and don't depart without unearthing the area's other secret garden, accessed via a discreet doorway in the square's north-eastern corner.

SW8
Nearest station: Vauxhall
bonningtonsquaregarden.org.uk

29
GREENWICH FOOT TUNNEL

Sub-Thames pedestrian pathway

Sure, the DLR is fun – but what about traversing the Thames through a delightfully spooky, subaquatic passageway? Built to serve south London-dwelling Victorian dock workers, this now criminally underused foot tunnel abounds with old-world magic – its glazed tile interior and magnificent domed entrance have stayed largely untouched since it opened in 1902. Cycling is prohibited, but the five- to ten-minute hike is worth it for the atmosphere alone. Combine it with some animal magic at the 32-acre Mudchute Farm and a mooch around Greenwich's copious historic wonders, like The Painted Hall (no.30) and Skittle Alley (no.34), or Cutty Sark and the Prime Meridian.

Nearest stations: Cutty Sark, Island Gardens
royalgreenwich.gov.uk

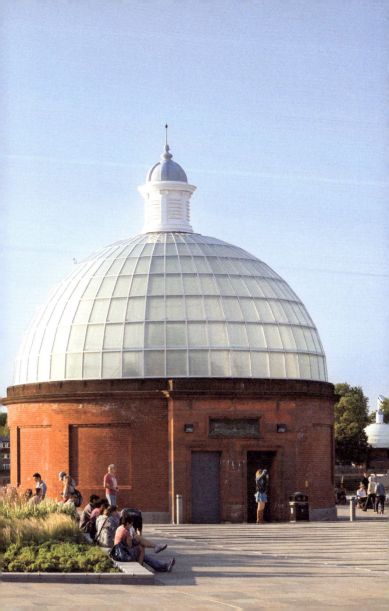

SOUTH

30
THE PAINTED HALL

'Britain's Sistine Chapel'

Hordes of long-suffering tourists snake through St. Peter's Square on the daily, all vying for a glimpse of the Sistine Chapel's ceiling. Meanwhile in Greenwich, Sir James Thornhill's answer to Michelangelo's masterpiece attracts a rather more modest crowd – though it's hard to see why. Painted in the early 1700s over a 19-year period, this epic baroque mural with a cast of 200 exquisitely rendered characters cavorting across a 3,700-square-metre canopy is a sight to behold. Best experienced horizontally on one of the hall's leather daybeds, the hypnotising frieze stars monarchs from the time, personifications of the four then-known continents and the artist himself. Join the mailing list for discounted tickets, otherworldly yoga classes and electrifying art installations beneath the ceiling.

Old Royal Naval College, College Way, SE10 9NN
Nearest station: Cutty Sark
ornc.org

31
CROSSNESS PUMPING STATION

Victorian 'cathedral of sewage'

God bless the Victorians, a society so repulsed by the idea of human waste they built giant baroque cathedrals to conceal their pumping stations. Plonked in the corner of a vast modern treatment works on the southern bank of the Thames, this now defunct structure might initially seem more haunting than handsome, but its relatively unremarkable shell conceals a spectacularly beautiful interior – one that, with its ornamental cast ironwork, could rival the most ornate churches. Check the website for details of upcoming guided tours and steaming days, when the world's largest rotative beam engine dramatically springs to life. And make sure to arrive in style, courtesy of the free heritage shuttle bus and enchanting narrow-gauge railway.

Bazalgette Way, SE2 9AQ
Nearest station: Abbey Wood
crossness.org.uk

32
CHISLEHURST CAVES

Lamplit tours of an underground labyrinth

What links mining, mushrooms and rock 'n' roll? Ordinarily, not a lot. But then this little-known subterranean labyrinth is hardly ordinary, with its 22 miles of tunnels – all painstakingly hand-excavated over hundreds of years. Believed to have been used for mining since the 13th century, the caves are said to date back more than 8,000 years – though arguably it's their recent history that's most alluring. The tiny church and hospital built by some 15,000 souls seeking shelter during the Blitz are still in situ, brought back to life by a band of merry mannequins. There's also still evidence of the stage where Pink Floyd and David Bowie once performed though, thankfully, not of the mushroom farm that was once here almost 100 years ago.

Caveside Close, Old Hill, BR7 5NL
Nearest station: Chislehurst
chislehurst-caves.co.uk

33
SANDS FILMS STUDIO

Idiosyncratic movie studio with film club

You've heard of Ealing and Elstree, but this charming Docklands film-production facility has somehow flown under the radar for nearly half a century, despite creating costumes for innumerable historical blockbusters – most recently 2019's *Little Women* and 2023's *Napoleon*. Occupying a late 18th-century warehouse in Rotherhithe, this Tardis-like studio is a period drama fan's wildest dream, with hand-sewn costumes stuffed in every corner and peculiar props strewn around like ornaments. Guided tours are by appointment, while the adjoining (and completely analogue) picture research library is open to all. However, it's the weekly cinema club, playing cult clasics in a tiny, armchair-filled room, and the sparkling concerts in the 100-seat baroque theatre, where the Sands magic really happens.

82 Saint Marychurch Street, SE16 4HZ
Nearest station: Rotherhithe
sandsfilms.co.uk

SOUTH

34
SKITTLE ALLEY AT ORNC

Enchanting Victorian bowling lanes

If you like your bowling alleys with two-tone shoes and slushies, you'd probably best stick to Finsbury Park's famously tacky Rowans. If, however, you're game for something a little different (and a little less kitsch), this 150-year-old skittle run might be right up your alley. Concealed in a long, vaulted basement room beneath the Old Royal Naval College chapel, these two strikingly well-preserved lanes were originally built for the ex-navy sailors who lived on-site, with old ships' timber used for flooring and practice cannonballs repurposed as bowling balls. A precursor to modern bowling, the nine-pin skittle alley might lack the bells, whistles and mechanisms of today's game, but strikes are just as satisfying. Even when you have to collect the balls yourself.

Old Royal Naval College, College Way, SE10 9NN
Nearest station: Greenwich
ornc.org/explore-whats-here/skittle-alley

35
THE ONION GARDEN

Not-for-profit urban green space

The name might sound a little acerbic, but rest assured you'll be all smiles (and no tears) upon discovering this little-known community garden, which sprouted from a previously dilapidated sliver of land behind Westminster City Hall. Conceived by local florist Jens Jakobsen, AKA Chief Onion, as the 'Hanging Gardens of Westminster', this pocket-sized oasis boasts more than 200 species of plants spanning fruit trees to wildflowers – and yes, there's oodles of onions. Grab a glass of wine from the storybook-cute cafe and savour it among the trees and tiny blackboards proffering upbeat snippets of wisdom. If the weather's rather less optimistic than the advice, opt for coffee and an apple Danish in the tranquil orangery.

5 Seaforth Place, SW1E 6AB
Nearest station: St James's Park
theoniongarden.org.

36
BASEMENT SATE

Drinks and desserts in an underground den

Soho has a long history of sating appetites in basements, so the sign refuting the presence of sex workers at this discreet subterranean establishment feels fitting. That said, its interiors are certainly not without their allure – all black leather seating, exposed brick and candlelight so dim you'll need your phone torch to decipher the equally alluring drinks menu. Quench your thirst with a gratifyingly fiery mezcal-infused Tongue Twister or a delightfully fruity Made in Ecuador. Then satisfy your sweet tooth (the food menu is exclusively so) with an exotic colada pudding or molten chocolate lava cake – or some other unspeakably naughty dessert.

8 Broadwick Street, W1F 8HN
Nearest station: Tottenham Court Road
basementsate.com

37
THE LITTLE BLUE DOOR

House party meets cocktail bar

Torn between heading out on the town and staying in with your feet up? Have your cocktail *and* drink it at the Little Blue Door, a surreptitious concept bar cosplaying as an eclectic, urban apartment. Nestled behind an inconspicuous ultramarine door on the Fulham Road, this playful home-from-home hosts everything from boozy bottomless brunches to DJ-led house parties where guests can explore the full run of the flat – laundry room and all. And if you're still tempted by a night in, perhaps the teacup cocktails, fully stocked games room and champagne vending machine can lure you out of your PJs?

871–873 Fulham Road, SW6 5HP
Nearest station: Parsons Green
thelittlebluedoor.co.uk

38
THE VAULT

Playful speakeasy with innovative cocktails

A bar buried behind a bookcase might sound insufferably gimmicky, but this bare-brick Soho cocktail den is definitely not one to shelve. Tucked below Milroy's – a 60-year-old whiskey store – the cosy, candlelit spot showcases an impressive assortment of guest scotches, bourbons and Japanese whiskies by way of its ever-evolving signature cocktail menu – though there'll be plenty else to entice you if whiskey's not your dram. Book ahead to guarantee a table, especially on Mondays when the raucous live jazz helps the herbaceous seasonal martinis and smoky old fashioneds go down – and makes that bookcase a darn sight easier to find.

3 Greek Street, W1D 4NX
Nearest station: Tottenham Court Road
instagram.com/thevault_soho

39
LIU XIAOMIAN AT THE JACKALOPE

Hot noods beneath a mews boozer

A jackalope is a little-known mythical mash-up of a jackrabbit (a type of hare) and an antelope. This similarly obscure Marylebone boozer blends comparably random concepts (a Chongqing noodle bar and a real ale pub) into something strangely beautiful – and, thankfully, 100 per cent real. Once you've located the clandestine mews, identified the 18th-century boozer and elbowed your way past the bar and down through its bowels, ask for a steaming bowl of xiaomian wheat noodles to consume in the restaurant or upstairs in the pub, then proceed to ladle it into your face until your soul is restored. Beware, these noods will blow your head off, so be sure to grab a pint (or a Chinese iced tea) to help them down.

The Jackalope, 43 Weymouth Mews, W1G 7EQ
Nearest station: Regent's Park
liu-xiaomian.com

40

CAHOOTS UNDERGROUND

Spirited 1940s-themed bar

Careless talk costs lives, so don't yell about this playful postwar-themed cocktail bar, which occupies a (real) WWII bomb shelter while posing as the (fake) abandoned Kingly Court Tube station. Instead, discreetly locate the sign for 'underground', have a quiet word with the 'station staff' and then descend the old-school wooden escalator to the atmospheric 'platforms' where a proper cockney knees-up awaits – 1946-style. Pick your pew: leather platform banquette or a perfectly upholstered train-carriage booth. Then select your concoction from the newspaper-style menu, be it a Blitzy, Marmite-infused twist on a bloody Mary or a juicy gin pick-me-up named after Vera Lynn (and disconcertingly served in a cup shaped like her head).

13 Kingly Court, W1B 5PW
Nearest station: Piccadilly Circus
Other locations: Borough
cahoots.co.uk

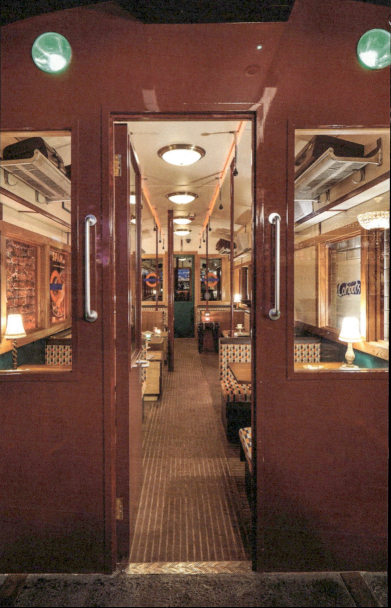

41
JUNO OMAKASE

Chef-curated sushi banquet

Small spaces and set menus aren't everyone's idea of fun, but daring diners will go loco for this Mexican-inspired omakase experience. Playing out in a tiny six-person restaurant-within-a-restaurant, this colourful culinary adventure is part feast, part theatre, with participants required to 'leave it up to (the chef)' – as per omakase's translation – to magic up a 15-course, sashimi-based banquet before their very eyes. Bone marrow-drizzled wagyu beef, carpaccioed red bream seasoned with flying ant and golden-eye snapper sprinkled with chapuline (dried, roasted grasshopper) are just a few of Oaxaca-trained chef Leonard Tanyag's surprising specialities, which go down particularly well with a bespoke sake flight, courtesy of the dedicated sommelier. Well, when in Japan...

Inside Los Mochis, 2–4 Farmer Street, W8 7SN
Nearest station: Notting Hill Gate
losmochis.co.uk

42
LA BODEGA NEGRA

Tequila and tacos in a secret cellar

If it's butt plugs and blindfolds you're after, you'd be better off ignoring the sleazy neon ads for strip tease and peep show adorning the frontage of this Soho spot's sleazy neon promises and trying Walker's Court instead. If, however, you harbour wild fantasies about prawn-stuffed corn tortillas with honeyed pineapple salsa, tangy leche de tigre salmon ceviche and fruity Jalapeño Mezcalitas, you've come to the right place. Keep (ahem) abreast of their Instagram page for news of racy drag brunches, raunchy cabaret, stimulating DJ sets and plenty more to whet your appetite.

9 Old Compton Street, W1D 5JF
Nearest stations: Tottenham Court Road, Leicester Square
labodeganegra.com

43
SECRET SANDWICH SHOP

Serious sandos served in a fabled night spot

Devotees of the Notting Hill party scene may be familiar with the legendary late-night dive bar the Globe. By day, this colourful venue bears witness to rather less raucous activities – namely the construction of sandwiches so fat their creators are apparently too embarrassed to advertise them. Inspired by Japanese *wanpaku* (naughty) 'sandos', these doorstop delights bookend criminal quantities of filling with thick and fluffy shokupan bread, served in a resealable box for when your stomach inevitably surrenders. The Hungry Dane is a meat lover's fantasy, but it's the synonymous Secret Sandwich – a veggie-stuffed epic of jaw-breaking proportions – that's really worth shouting about.

103 Talbot Road, W11 2AT
Nearest station: Westbourne Park
secretsandwichshop.com

44
THE LITERARIUM AT THIRD MAN RECORDS

Blind book vending machine inside a music shop

With its safety-yellow facade, Jack White's indie record store is hardly inconspicuous – but what lies in its atmospheric basement is rather more mysterious. Resembling a customised 1950s refrigerator, this book vending machine randomly dispenses everything from poetry and short story collections, to anonymous manifestoes and opening chapters of yet-to-be-published novels – all lovingly assembled and bound in-store. Literary lottery players need simply purchase two tokens from the upstairs till, locate the Literarium in the Blue Basement and drop them in the slot to be rewarded with a satisfying clunk and a mystery tome. If that isn't enough to entice you, check out the straight-to-vinyl recording booth and exclusive White Stripes merch.

1 Marshall Street, W1F 9BA
Nearest station: Piccadilly Circus
thirdmanrecords.com

45
ATTENDANT COFFEE ROASTERS

Specialty coffee in a Victorian loo

Feeling… flush? Spend a penny or two at this undercover cafe, where the speciality coffees and indulgent all-day breakfasts are anything but bog standard. Housed in a converted men's public toilet, the appropriately named Attendant has retained many of its original fixtures, from glossy wall and floor tiles to the Doulton & Co. porcelain urinals, now cleverly repurposed as seating partitions. Order a seasonal latte (be it a revitalising iced chocolate in the warmer months or a comforting blueberry matcha for autumn) alongside one of their signature bacon brioche buns with *all* the trimmings. You'd be potty to miss it.

27A Foley Street, W1W 6DY
Nearest station: Oxford Circus
the-attendant.com

46
POETRY PHARMACY

Words for wellness

Sometimes the only medicine that will do is a pertinent poem (and maybe a slice of cake). That's the idea behind The Poetry Pharmacy, a curative bookshop and cafe hiding in plain sight on Europe's busiest shopping street, inside Lush's flagship store. Poetry anthologies are themed by sentiment, as this 'alternative therapy' hotspot dispenses prescriptions tailored to very specific ailments. Poetry cuttings pertain to empty-nest syndrome, existential angst and heartbreak, coiled up into capsules and sold in pill bottles for emergency consumption. Once you've collected your literary linctus, proceed to the 'Dispensary' cafe for a restorative cuppa and something sweet enough to alleviate any malady.

1st floor, Lush, 175–179 Oxford Street, W1D 2JS
Nearest station: Oxford Circus
poetrypharmacy.co.uk

47
HYDE PARK PET CEMETERY

Victorian animal burial ground

Hyde Park could be called Hide Park, so numerous are its secrets. Did you know, for example, that its hidden greenhouse cultivates almost all the Royal Parks' plants, or that there's a tiny art gallery inside the Wellington Arch? Its most stirring surprise, though, lurks on its northern edge, in a gatekeeper's cottage garden only accessible via infrequent Royal Parks tours. Said to be the first public pet cemetery in the UK, the strangely charming plot is the final resting place of more than 1,000 domestic animals – most belonging to well-to-do locals. Some tiny tombstone inscriptions are more comprehensible than others (burials date back to 1880), but look out for Cherry, the cemetery's first inhabitant, and Balu, its only murder victim.

41 Bayswater Road, W2 4RQ
Nearest station: Lancaster Gate
royalparks.org.uk

48
LIDO GARDEN

Hyde Park's seasonal secret

One might question the virtue of a 'secret' garden inside what is already one of London's most expansive green spaces, but on a sizzling summer's day when Hyde Park's cafes are heaving and its playgrounds hellish, this shady spot feels like a tiny piece of paradise. Open from April to September in concurrence with the adjacent Serpentine Lido, this little-known utopia packs in a small but sweet under-5s playground and plenty of al fresco seating where rustic pizzas and barbecue bits are served all summer, and punchy frozen margaritas keep flowing long after the Serpentine Lido Cafe has run dry. Enter via the lido footbridge for VIP vibes, or through the hole in the hedge for more of a Secret Garden experience.

Hyde Park, W2 2UH
Nearest station: Knightsbridge

49
SMITH'S COURT

Intimate square with independent shops

Quiet corners are hard to come by in Soho. Follow the playtime shrieks from the area's only primary school, though, before quickly dipping down the alley opposite, and you're in for a tranquil treat. Once home to stables, farriers and blacksmith workshops, this recently redeveloped courtyard retains much of its traditional character. Multi-paned shop windows complement characterful cobblestone, with independent businesses hawking everything from handmade chocolates to artisanal eyewear. Head here on your lunch break for uplifting boxed salads from Bibi's, impromptu massages from Walk-In Backrub and matchless inner-London village vibes.

W1D 7DW
Nearest station: Piccadilly Circus

50

SHEPHERDESS WALK MOSAICS

Classically inspired community murals

Blink and you'd miss the tiny artwork that signposts these Hoxton treasures. Buried in the northernmost corner of Shepherdess Walk Park, Tessa Hunkin's Romanesque mosaics are best approached from the street, via the splendidly eerie passageway that tunnels beneath the adjacent Georgian terrace – making their discovery all the more rewarding. Assembled by Hunkin and around 150 local volunteers in honour of the London 2012 Olympics, the panels depict seasonal scenes from modern Hackney life while masquerading as ancient Roman relics. Look out for the giveaway electric leaf blower and mobile phones, as well as the shepherdesses that gave the street and park – once a well-trodden route to market – its name.

N1 7QA
Nearest station: Old Street
hackney-mosaic.co.uk

NORTH

51
CAMDEN PASSAGE

Independent shopping street

Upper Street has its charms, but it's the cobbled alley behind it that's the real beating heart of Angel. Like a smaller, stealthier Portobello Road, this slender thoroughfare throbs with independent spirit, filled with colourful boutiques selling vintage clothing, quirky homeware and artisan foods. Twice a week, market stalls also peddle everything from costume jewellery to mantle dogs. Fuel up at Redemption Roasters then proceed north to Inca or Magpie for a rummage through their retro threads, then onto Loop for contemporary knitting supplies. Wolf down a spicy, eggy kottu roti at Trampoline, before having a mosey around Moosey's latest art show, finishing with some treasure hunting around the eclectic market stalls.

N1 8EA
Nearest station: Angel
camdenpassageislington.co.uk

NORTH

52
BAPS SHRI SWAMINARAYAN MANDIR

Traditional Hindu stone temple

Otherwise known as the Neasden Temple, this sumptuous marble structure is hardly inconspicuous, yet surprisingly few Londoners are aware of its existence – and even fewer know that it's free to visit any day of the week, regardless of your spiritual inclination. However loose your handle on Hinduism, the mandir's knowledgeable swamis (monks) will gladly reveal its secrets, from mesmerising arti light rituals in the Maha-Mandap (Great Hall) to the breathtaking ornamental flower garden. Plan ahead to ensure you don't miss anything, and set aside time for a post-mooch feast in the on-site vegetarian restaurant – another open secret that's not to be overlooked.

Pramukh Swami Road, NW10 8HW
Nearest station: Stonebridge Park
londonmandir.baps.org

53
ST JOHN'S LODGE GARDEN

Royal Park's serene secret

'Inner Circle' is a fitting address for this surreptitious spot – originally the grounds of one of The Regent's Park's grandest villas. While the house is private, the garden has been open to all since 1928 – though that doesn't stop a mooch around its labyrinthine 'rooms' from feeling delightfully illicit. Invariably empty (the gated entrance is far from conspicuous) and deemed 'fit for meditation' by its designer, landscape architect Robert Weir Shultz, the 35,250-square-foot plot feels significantly more secluded than the surrounding park – making it ideal for contemplative wanders. Look out for the magnificent bronze sculptures, gigantic stone urns and Victorian-style flowerbeds that give each of the hedge-walled compartments their own character.

Inner Circle, NW1 4NR
Nearest station: Regent's Park
royalparks.org.uk

54
CONSERVATORY ARCHIVES

Botanical paradise

The name 'garden centre' spectacularly undersells Conservatory Archives, a concept plant store for which 'untamed utopia' or 'rainforest portal' feel infinitely more apt. Both of its sites could easily have been plucked from a children's fantasy novel, but the Islington store is by far the most impressive, inhabiting a magical Victorian stable buried down a discreet alley. Specimens err on the exotic, from the velvety-leafed Philodendron melanochrysum to white-flecked variegated monsteras, and are unsystematically arranged to create the sense of ambling through a forest. Admittedly you won't find much in the way of gardening accessories here, but the surprisingly inexpensive planters are top of the pots.

3 Middleton Mews, N7 9LT
Nearest station: Caledonian Road
Other locations: Clapton
conservatoryarchives.co.uk

NORTH

55
THE HILL GARDEN AND PERGOLA

Faded grandeur on Hampstead Heath

Once the extensive gardens of a wealthy soap merchant's pile, the hauntingly beautiful Hill Garden and Pergola is Hampstead's best-kept secret, occupying a covert position behind atmospheric woodland on the secluded West Heath. Derelict for decades, the Edwardian-era folly has been painstakingly restored, though with its vine-swathed Italianate walkway and overgrown flora it still feels like the mysterious remnants of a lost civilisation. Begin your visit with a scenic wander through the historic streets of Hampstead Village, winding your way up Heath Street via the pergola and woods, before settling down with a fireside pint at the deliciously spooky Spaniards Inn.

Inverforth Close, NW3 7EX
Nearest station: Hampstead
cityoflondon.gov.uk

56
PARKLAND WALK

Idiosyncratic nature reserve on an old railway

Abandoned train platforms, a chewing-gum art trail and London's very own bat cave; this three-mile-long nature reserve isn't just delightfully secluded, it's also charmingly bonkers. Tracing the route of a former railway line linking Finsbury Park to Alexandra Palace, the verdant walking route will lead you past heavily graffitied railway arches and even an epic adventure playground, but still affords the sense of having completely escaped urbanity – at least for a couple of hours. End your amble with a tipple at Finsbury Park's Faltering Fullback or Highgate's Boogaloo (both suitably eccentric) – but not before you've bid adieu to the walk's equally apt mascot, the spriggan, a little-known mythical creature recognised for its propensity to guard buried treasure.

Nearest stations: Highgate, Finsbury Park
parkland-walk.org.uk

NORTH

57
QUEEN'S WOOD

Ancient woodland with fairy-tale cafe

If you go down to Queen's Wood today, you're in for a big surprise. Highgate Wood's wilder, less famous next-door neighbour is full of spooky secrets, from a cafe straight out of Grimm's fairy tales to a long history of pagan rituals, and even talk of a 17th-century plague pit lurking beneath the soil. Still, it's not all magic and folklore at this gorgeously unkempt nature reserve, where anemones and buttercups convene in tangles between the ancient oaks and hornbeams, and song thrushes and woodpeckers chirrup overhead. The cafe's popularity has swelled in recent months and early birds catch the worm – or, in this case, the pistachio pain au chocolat – so head down first-thing for some much-needed pre-ramble fuel.

Queen's Wood Road, N6 6UU
Nearest station: Highgate
fqw.org.uk

IMAGE CREDITS

Crossness Pumping Station © Arcaid Images / Alamy; Greenwich Foot Tunnel © John Keeble; The Hill Garden and Pergola © Marco Kessler; Larry's © Melissa Coppola; Ümit & Son © Orrin Saint-Pierre; Hidden Underground Tours © LTM; Lounge Bohemia © David Turecky; Hidden Underground Tours © LTM; Mail Rail © The Postal Museum; Larry's © Melissa Coppola; Katsute100 © David Post; Cecil Court © Alex Segre / Alamy; Dans Le Noir © Dans Le Noir?; Open House © Andrew Too Boon Tan / Getty; London's Roman Amphitheatre, first image © Jamie Smith, second image © Nick Harrison / Alamy; The Post Building Roof Garden © David Post; The Artist's Garden, first image © Waldemar Sikora / Alamy, second image © Malcolm Park / Alamy; Lounge Bohemia © David Turecky; Sessions Arts Club © Louise Long; Postman's Park © Marco Kessler; Barbican Conservatory © Taran Wilkhu; London Open Gardens © Cate Gillon / Getty; Rochelle Canteen © Helen Cathcart; The Natural Philosopher Cocktail Bar © David Post; Jack the Ripper Tour © Tim George; Trinity Buoy Wharf Lighthouse, first image © Nathaniel Noir / Alamy, second image © James Whitaker; Dennis Severs' House © Charlotte Schreiber; Viktor Wynd Museum of Curiosities © Oskar Proctor; Rooftop Saunas © Nick Howe; The Approach Gallery, first and second image © FXP PHOTOGRAPHY, third image (Kira Freije, meteorites, 2022) © Michael Brzezinski. Courtesy of the artist and The Approach, London; Ümit & Son © Orrin Saint-Pierre; Dalston Eastern Curve Garden, first image © Charlotte Schreiber, second image © Martin Usborne; Eel Pie Island, first image © Lois GoBe second image © Micky Lee / Alamy; WC Wine & Charcuterie © David Post; Bonnington Square © David Post; Greenwich Foot Tunnel, first image © Robert Harding / Alamy, second image © Daniel Greenhouse / Alamy; The Painted Hall © Old Royal Naval College; Crossness Pumping Station © Peter Scrimshaw; Chislehurst Caves © Kumar Sriskandan / Alamy; Sands Films Studio © Tony Farrugia; Skittle Alley at ORNC © James Brittain / VIEW / Alamy image © Nick Harrison / Alamy; The Onion Garden © David Post; Basement Sate @ chefromainrocher; The Little Blue Door © Bianka London; The Vault, Milroy's © Rusne Draz, courtesy of The Vault; Liu Xiaomian at The Jackalope © David Post; Cahoots © Johnny Stephens; Juno Omakase © Carla Barber; La Bodega Negra © Ricker Restaurant Group; Secret Sandwich Shop © Marcus Patrick Brown; The Literarium at Third Man Records © David Post; Attendant Coffee Roasters © Nathaniel Noir / Alamy; Poetry Pharmacy © Hayden Kitson; Hyde Park Pet Cemetery © Zoontar GmbH / Alamy; Lido Garden © Adam Luszniak; Smith's Court © Nathaniel Noir / Alamy; Shepherdess Walk Mosaics © Lucinda de Jasay; Camden Passage © Chanel Irvine; BAPS Shri Swaminarayan Mandir © Taran Wilkhu; St John's Lodge Garden © Marco Kessler; Conservatory Archives © Conservatory Archives Ltd IG @conservatory_archives; The Hill Garden and Pergola © Marco Kessler; Parkland Walk © Marco Kessler; Queen's Wood © Marco Kessler.

An Opinionated Guide to Secret London
First edition

Published in 2025 by Hoxton Mini Press, London
Copyright © Hoxton Mini Press 2025. All rights reserved.

Text by Emmy Watts
Editing by Zoë Jellicoe
Production Design by Dom Grant
Proofreading by Florence Ward

With thanks to Matthew Young for initial series design.

Please note: we recommend checking the websites listed for each
entry before you visit for the latest information on price, opening times
and pre-booking requirements.

The right of Emmy Watts to be identified as the creator of this Work
has been asserted under the Copyright, Designs and Patents Act 1988.

Thank you to all of the individuals and institutions who have provided images
and arranged permissions. While every effort has been made to trace the present
copyright holders we apologise in advance for any unintentional omission or error,
and would be pleased to insert the appropriate acknowledgement in any
subsequent edition.

No part of this publication may be reproduced, stored in a retrieval system,
or transmitted in any form or by any means, electronic, mechanical, photocopying,
recording or otherwise, without the prior written permission
of the copyright owner.

A CIP catalogue record for this book is available from the British Library.

ISBN: 978-1-914314-87-2

Printed and bound by OZGraf, Poland

Hoxton Mini Press is an environmentally conscious publisher, committed
to offsetting our carbon footprint. This book is 100 per cent carbon compensated,
with offset purchased from Stand For Trees.

Every time you order from our website, we plant a tree:
www.hoxtonminipress.com

Selected opinionated guides in the series:

For more go to www.hoxtonminipress.com

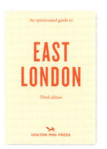

INDEX

The Approach Gallery, 23
The Artist's Garden, 10
Attendant Coffee Roasters, 45
BAPS Shri Swaminarayan Mandir, 52
Basement Sate, 36
Barbican Conservatory, 14
La Bodega Negra, 42
Bonnington Square, 28
Cahoots Underground, 40
Camden Passage, 51
Cecil Court, 5
Conservatory Archives, 54
Dalston Eastern Curve Garden, 25
Chislehurst Caves, 32
Crossness Pumping Station, 31
Dans Le Noir?, 6
Dennis Severs' House, 20
Eel Pie Island, 26
Greenwich Foot Tunnel, 29
Hidden London Tours, 1

The Hill Garden and Pergola, 55
Hyde Park Pet Cemetery, 47
Jack the Ripper Tour, 18
Juno Omakase, 41
Katsute100, 4
Larry's, 3
Lido Garden, 48
The Literarium at Third Man Records, 44
The Little Blue Door, 37
Liu Xiaomian at The Jackalope, 39
London Open Gardens, 15
London's Roman Amphitheatre, 8
Lounge Bohemia, 11
Mail Rail, 2
The Natural Philosopher, 17
The Onion Garden, 35
Open House, 7
The Painted Hall, 30
Parkland Walk, 56
Poetry Pharmacy, 46
The Post Building Roof Garden, 9
Postman's Park, 13

Queen's Wood, 57
Rochelle Canteen, 16
Rooftop Saunas, 22
Sands Films Studio, 33
Secret Sandwich Shop, 43
Sessions Arts Club, 12
Shepherdess Walk Mosaics, 50
Smith's Court, 49
Skittle Alley at ORNC, 34
St John's Lodge Garden, 53
Trinity Buoy Wharf, 19
Ümit & Son, 24
The Vault, 38
The Viktor Wynd Museum of Curiosities, 21
WC Wine & Charcuterie, 27